THE POWER OF ZERO THINKING

REWIRING THOUGHT PROCESS

V PRAVEEN RAJ

ISBN

Hardcase 979-8-89519-530-7
Paperback 979-8-89475-334-8

Disclaimer

The author does not claim any original idea of this concept called Zero Thinking. He is attempting to re-interpret the existing wisdom passed down from ages towards understanding of human thinking and man's progress towards realizing his self. He may inadvertently use thoughts from other authors and may have overlooked their contribution by not mentioning their name. The idea is to convey message beneficial to the society in general.

Contents

Contents

Preface

It was one Sunday evening I was sitting on a couch watching a movie and then suddenly my wife comes over tells me to get up and get ready to go out.

"Where I asked"

"We are going to the pilgrim booking office to register" She said.

"Oh come on, today is Sunday, just leave me alone we can go some other day"

"Fifteen minutes, we are leaving" she just commanded with no intention to go back on her decision.

"I think the office may not be open on Sundays, don't you think so?"

"They are closed only on Tuesdays"

I said "It is already 4 pm; I feel the office might have closed for the day"

"Will you please get up and be ready? The counters are open till 6.00PM" she went on.

"Okay, I will get ready in few minutes"

We were on the road driving with our son sitting behind quietly wondering where we all were going. My mood was little irritated as I was pulled out from relaxing position watching an interesting movie. I have had few similar experiences before therefore, preferred to keep bit silent. However, old habits die hard so I just broke the conversation.

"If I find the counters closed then you are responsible for spoiling my Sunday evening" I asserted. She didn't bother and just remained silent listening to songs being played on our car audio.

Before I could understand anything further, I had a flash of wisdom dawning on me. I asked myself 'Why should I pick any argument with my wife, when I already agreed to take her to the pilgrim booking centre?' What will I gain in raking up the issue which I am sure will lead to unpleasant situation? An argument may break resulting in bitter fight. Should I really do something that may lead to a bad day OR shall I exercise little patience and make the day better for all. The inner ego was constantly triggering me to square up the situation. Why not I do something opposite? Instead of trying to outsmart her why not join her in the mission. After all she was doing something good for every one of us, so why treat this situation the other way? So, I BLANKED MY THOUGHTS TO ZERO. I visualized that we are entering the office and registering our names for the temple visit. The next twenty minutes went by without any other negative thought but focussed on driving to the registration office and to reach in time. As we reached the office, I asked my son and wife to get down so that I could park the car and come. I reached the counters and the time on the clock showed 5.45 PM and the closing time is 6.00. I prayed that the queue shouldn't be long and we should do our registration.

Surprisingly, there were hardly few people standing in front of the counter. The registration was done successfully and my wife was delighted to get the dates that she asked for. I too was happy and relieved.

Just an hour ago, I was feeling bad and what happened next surprised me a lot. My wife was in happier mood and she suggested going to a restaurant before we could head home. I made her happy and satisfied (a dream of most husbands) something more challenging than starting a company. I began to find out what changed the whole situation and what is this Zero Thinking? Actually, it was more to do with emotions than thinking. I discovered this method and started practicing it with some amazing results. This is not anything new and is already in practice I just coined this term ZERO THINKING to remind myself to enforce it whenever I needed it. Some are gifted in using this method often and goes by the term like patience, avoiding judgments, holding on to any impulsive decisions, not to react to anything quickly etc. I just needed some kind of term to remind myself that will quickly make me take control of the situation. It was the beginning of the journey in pondering the benefits of this ZERO THINKING in every situation one comes across.

There are many who apply this method and I have just structured it to various situations to discover a new way to find peace with self and exploring life more meaningfully. Actually, I had no clue to handle even a small crisis and used to get emotional. I always envied those who remained unusually calm and lead quite successful life. What was their SECRET? Well, I tried explaining as much as I can in the following chapters. It is not an instant solution to any problem but requires patience to apply the methods. This book requires constant reference and re-reading to understand the content more deeply to provide lasting effect. The idea is not to follow anything blindly but to find one's own solution through the help of techniques provided.

All the best and happy reading!!!

CHAPTER 1

Back to Basics: Importance of Focus

Much water has flowed through every perennial river around the world and we humans (most of them) have lost the ability to focus on one thing for a longer duration. We are either distracted by a phone call, social media notification or a barrage of WhatsApp and email messages. We have not only developed fear of losing something by not attending to those notifications but get paranoid if we are not close to our gadgets. This has robbed one of the most precious gifts of humans and that is the ability to focus on given task without interruptions. The inefficiency of the output has been suitably compensated by the tools available. For example, instead of searching through pages of book for particular information, the same can be obtained through search from the internet. It doesn't matter if one is not glued to the book for longer duration and they also do not bother about small distractions.

So, one may ask what is the big deal? Why do we need the ability to focus for a specific period of time when half of our tasks get completed with the help of tools and gadgets available around us? Fine, that is the good answer! But wait!!

Do you know the power of focus?

Do you understand the impact of concentration on any result?

Do you agree that the edge over other competitors is better with the help of steady focus?

Do you know that the quality of result is better achieved through focused effort?

If your answer is yes for all of the above, then you need to proceed further to know the art of focusing better by avoiding distractions through a planned effort. I can vouch that the greatest asset of this century would be the ability to focus on a single subject for a longer duration of time without getting distracted even by thoughts. Yes, I mean thoughts. You may conveniently keep yourself away from all the gadgets like phone etc. but will you be able to control your thoughts to keep that focus laser sharp? The single biggest distraction is OUR MIND followed by other outside disturbances. It is also one of the most challenging and difficult part of human behavior to achieve total mind control.

The idea is to assess your focusing ability by reading a book. If you can manage to read a page of any normal sized book without taking your concentration away from the contents, then you have good focus. Some people may read without actually understanding what they are reading. Such readers actually complete the reading but unable to recall the contents properly or even able to understand properly what they have read. If one is facing such a situation, then the person is having poor concentration and needs exercise to focus more sharply for longer duration. The most important thing to contain is the mind. Like they say put your mind, heart and soul into what you are doing. In order to practice this, one should go back to school days of opening the text and reading it completely with understanding. Initially, start with the paragraph and read again and again till you completely understand what is written.

Reading should not be like reading a list but reading a sentence in order to understand what is written. It doesn't matter in what language you read, the thing is to READ FIRST to focus better.

The next step is to write what you read immediately after you finished reading. Find out how much you can recall and at what level. You don't need to by heart the whole text but to deeply understand every word and the sentence. You can re-write what you just read not necessarily word by word. You can rephrase the sentence the way one feels comfortable. The idea is to know whether you managed to focus without letting thoughts wonder. If you feel lazy to write, then at least try recall in mind the contents that you just read. Well, coming to this chapter that you are READING NOW, DID YOU FOLLOW WHAT I JUST SAID ABOVE? If not, then go back read again. Wait! Before you start reading, try blanking your thoughts from every activity that occupied your thinking. Be in the surroundings and don't let thoughts fly beyond your environment. Observe things around like lighting, window, curtains and whatever furniture around. Even listen to the noises around like traffic sound, TV audio, people speaking or even bird chirping. Just do this for at least five minutes in order to keep YOUR THOUGHTS EMPTY. Do not even analyze what you see, hear or smell just let the observations be restricted to each senses rather than allowing it to enter the brain. Feel your breath and your physical body. This is to keep the mind from exiting from the surroundings and landing in some fairy land. You can pause reading further...............

Did you feel the surge of unnecessary thoughts from your brain? You didn't wonder in your thoughts rather listened to the noise in the vicinity if there was one and also staring at walls around you and observing everything present inside the room. Start reading again. Once you are ready to read anything with concentration and understanding then proceed with further chapters. I have tried sequencing each chapter based on its importance.

This is not a one-time effort but rather an exercise to be performed routinely in order it to become a habit. If ten people are taught the skills of success only one is expected to be successful and it is mainly due to his or her ability to convert the learning into a habit by constantly sticking to the routine of doing again and again. This may sound little simple but one of the most difficult technique to acquire. One may wonder if every successful person had used this method. The answer is yes. There is a one set of people who have no option but forced into a situation of achieving results. The others are those who are not forced by any of the challenging situations but out of pure passion and will power to carry them to their goals. Both these type of people in different situations achieve victory in their missions. However, among the second category most people fail due to the 'comfort zone' factor which keeps most of them lazy. If you are the one who is in comfort zone and wish to achieve big success, then stay out of the cozy comforts of your present situation.

I will be guiding in each chapter on various topics whereby the application of ZT (Zero thinking) provides immense results. The power of Zero thinking is a quite simple exercise with wide range of benefits

Fix time for important tasks and stick to the schedule

Prepare desk every time while commencing the tasks before you actually sit down.

Keep the distractions away like phone

Keep a daily fixed schedule for specific tasks to create a consistency in progress

THINK ONLY ACTION ORIENTED THOUGHTS (this means the thoughts that occupy the mind should be predominantly the one that is fairly actionable not any fancy one. Further the thoughts should systematically be put on the path of action. If no action is taking place on some of the thoughts that had been occupying for quite some time, then it is time to eliminate that thought from the dominant position of mind. This way the mind is UNBURDENED of useless and non-actionable and non-progressive thoughts)

The above exercise translates into a HABIT and it is time consuming process. *Correct habits are more effective than forced efforts.*

Use the Power of Zero thinking by blanking all thoughts in the mind. Bring the mind to the immediate environment. For ex. If you are driving, then concentrate on the road and the traffic or if you are cooking then focus on the preparation till the dish is made. Stick to the immediate vicinity of your surroundings and don't let your mind wonder in past or in future. This zero thinking will also eliminate errors thus creating a zero defect work output.

CHAPTER 2

Law of Acceptance

As an ambitious young person, the eagerness to achieve was very high in me. My struggle ranged from academic to career building and eventually to making it big in business. Despite hard efforts and determination, I was not able to achieve any breakthrough in academics, career and enterprise. I felt like dismissing all the theories of will power, determination and hard work which leads one to success. It took many years to find out the real truth behind my struggle and the reasons for failing. After deep study of myself through constant assessment of my own ability, I was surprised to find out the few faults that I had, which I mention it below:

Hard work: In my own judgment I thought I was putting lot of hard work, however the realty being I wasn't putting a quality effort which means I wasn't going that EXTRA mile.

Focus: I was good at thinking and learning new things, which led me to find enthusiasm on a wide range of subjects. However, I seriously lacked focus on any one thing. The ability to focus deeply on organized action towards a specific useful purpose is a valuable asset. This is one of the tough areas to master and I lacked it badly.

Acceptance: Apart from above, the one BIG discovery I made was the ability to accept the things as they are. This is a natural quality in many people and helps them find peace within. I was a rebel, resisted failure and began thrusting my energy on overcoming each and every obstacle. On one hand I was increasing my will power and determination, but the end results weren't satisfactory. Every impediment and failure was UNACCEPTABLE to me. This left me frustrated most often. I was not only losing focus but also getting exhausted frequently. I learnt a powerful wisdom "What cannot be changed needs to be accepted". If a failure has occurred, then it needs to accepted and work towards avoiding a similar situation in future. The unacceptability will not allow you to LEARN the causes of failure. There is a need for tactical retreat. This doesn't mean to accept any unpleasant situation and relax but to learn from the mistakes and improve SKILLS to avoid it in future. I discovered the LAW OF ACCEPTANCE (LOA) through Zero Thinking method, whereby I continued blanking my thoughts and bringing my emotions under control. The Law of Acceptance teaches the powerful quality of humility and strengthens your inner self. The weak people accept many things meekly and never make any effort to improve. This isn't the law of acceptance but surrender. The LOA is the art of moving one step ahead of failure. One can allow negative emotion of anger and frustration at the first experience of failure but more important is to avoid over enthusiasm in handling the same. Don't push towards Positive Thinking to overcome a setback as that will create an artificial comfort zone which will not open up the faculty in mind to find concrete solutions. There is no such thing as celebration till the goal is achieved. One should accept the present situation in whatever form it is. It is easy to keep regretting things all the time like not having done something earlier that could have changed the course of life. First, one got to believe even if it is irrational that there are things which happen for no logical purpose. Why did this happen to me? One can keep pondering over it for years to come. One got to understand that there are no answers for it. It is better to avoid comparing ourselves with others. Each of us is unique in some way or the other. A fish is more suited to swim not to climb a tree. If you are a fish, then look for water don't attempt to climb a tree. Self-assessment is necessary to understand one's own strengths and abilities. All weaknesses can be overcome through constant effort assisted by experts and counsellors. Get guidance where necessary. The fact is that you are not a fish but a human so you have options so look for resources to strengthen your skills. You can either learn swimming or the rock climbing or both if one has resources. The idea is to know what is more suitable with the given resources. My son wanted to be a world class table tennis player but with the given resources I simply said that is next to impossible unless you moved into a place where world's best players are playing. It is essential to know one's position before nurturing any dreams. So begin by accepting your limits and then think of ways to go beyond those limits. If a way is found or possible then strive to get it or else abandon it and find different way to move ahead. Every tennis player dreams of winning the Wimbledon but only select few manage to get that coveted title. Some accept the fact and continue playing for the sake of passion and enjoyment even though they secretly dream of achieving it someday. The dreams are just a catalyst to keep going and success is not just achieving things but a journey to be enjoyed even if the destination doesn't arrive. One should remove obsession and replace it with passion in order to find inner strength. The desperate ones do accomplish things in the end but only to feel drained out later. This does not mean one should not strive to reach goals but avoid the attitude of desperation. Allow the nature to take care of things for you. Apply ZT by flushing out all such obsessions, frustrations and desperations. Blank your thoughts and emotions for more meaningful effort without bothering about the end results. Many weak players have overcome strong champions using this method. The wisdom is not in becoming the richest man but managing a strong business. The satisfaction can be found in various ways.

Happy ZERO thinking!!

CHAPTER 3

Elimination of Unwanted Habits (Bad Ones)

First, it is essential to list out as many bad habits as possible. There should not be any prejudice in admitting any of the bad habit. It is like telling the doctor the entire problem for him to start the treatment. Now, what constitutes a bad habit? Let us take the usual bad habits one may find it quite common as follows:

1. Procrastination

2. Laziness

3. Rising up late in the morning

4. Not maintaining proper hygiene

5. Telling lies

6. Feeling jealous of others

7. Hatred and contempt for no apparent reason

8. Short tempered

9. Speaking ill about others behind their back (gossip mongering)

10.   Ogling at others

11.   Watching porn

12.   Smoking

13.   Drinking excessively

14.   Excessive indulgence in sensual pleasures

15.   False promising (not keeping up word)

16.   Whining and complaining all the time

17.   Lack of empathy (insensitive to other's feelings)

18.   Indiscipline conduct (for ex. Insubordination)

19.   Excessive fear and phobia

20.   Always anxious about life and future

21.   Behaving indecently (making fun of others as well as being rude in conduct)

22.   Smart phone addiction.

23.   Doing unlawful activities

Above mentioned lists are some of the darker sides of bad habits. What about habits which are not bad but still considered part of problem in one's progress in life?

Here is the list of habits which may not be bad in the real sense but if practiced in excess can cause more harm:

Self-obsession

Feeling guilty all the time

Perfection in everything

Over discipline

Excessive affection towards loved ones

Lack of assertion (timidity)

Please all attitudes

Freaky habits (pointing faults, sniffing everything, OCD)

Falling into depressive thoughts

Excessive devotion in spiritual matters

Giving unwanted advices to others

Unwanted interference in other's matters

Over thinking and wild thoughts

Excessive reading with no tangible purpose

Gluttony and constant craving for something to eat

Feeling low for no apparent reason (lack of confidence and zero physical activity to keep fit)

Wasting time on non-important issues which causes forgetfulness, lack of clear vision and blurring of focus

Unorganized life style (lack of planning and purpose in life)

Cynicism (blaming society or establishment for all the ills)

Poor listening and over talking (especially about self)

Lack of will (giving up easily)

Poor greeting habits like not giving proper attention to people around or those who visit.

Watching TVs, browsing without purpose, social media activity and spending more time on Smartphone

Unnecessarily judging others (unwanted analysis of other's behaviors)

It will not be surprising to say that a single person can possess almost all of the above characteristics in small portion and no doubt that they are all blockages in pipes for success to flow smoothly. It is therefore, some of the reasons that despite having all the talents, qualities, hard work and tools that most people struggle to reach their desired goals.

Now the fundamental question: How hard is to overcome all the above weaknesses or habits?

As mentioned right in the beginning, one got to actually list out most pressing bad habits and plan to eliminate them altogether. Surely, it is not an easy task and interestingly it is also not very complicated. Just jot down answers next to these lists on methods of elimination. Most likely one can come with some answer or so. Self-learning is more effective than following other's methods.

There are different methods to break the bad habits. Most can be self learnt through auto suggestion.

Zero thinking is one ideal way to kick those stimulants that raises these thoughts which leads to incompatible behaviors. It is not easy to control the thoughts that dominate due to 'bad' habits cultivated over a period of time. Just as I mentioned, it is not the thoughts but stimulations that needs to be controlled. Try and keep the stimulations away before it re-ignites unwanted thoughts. There is something called passive sins. Here, you may not be actually committing anything wrong but constantly stimulate your thoughts in thinking about anything evil and bad. This is due to frustration over something and they find solace in indulgence what seems harmless evil thoughts. *An evil thought cannot be harmless; the first victim is you.* You are cultivating a stimulant that leads to unwanted thoughts eventually causing bad habits. It is comparatively easy to overcome the stimulants of mind than the thoughts. They are like small sparks that causes the fire called thoughts. So extinguish that spark in the beginning.

Try this again and again till you are in a commanding position to overcoming any type of bad habits. ZT is one of the methods that are helpful in purging out all the unwanted stimulants from the mind. However, one shouldn't be obsessed in winning every effort, at times things may spin out of control. Allow some 'disturbances' but make sure that you got to finally rein them in. There is no need to feel guilty in the process as every effort is worth taking.

Seeking help is useful in overcoming many bad habits. When we were young, our parents constantly reprimanded us on various things that they considered harmful. Once we grow into adults and feel independent, we tend to ignore many such habits which may appear harmless in the beginning. One got to engage someone in the family to prompt whoever is tempted to do unwanted things. I tell my spouse to remind me whenever I am on the 'wrong' path so as to immediately re-align myself back to the right track. The spouse should be given full powers to be strict and no leniency to be shown whatsoever. At times, the people involved, usually compromise on the common goals for the sake of immediate pleasure. Little relaxation may be okay but if principles are constantly compromised then there is no way to escape from various bad habits. Feel better and reward yourself every time you overcome any habit that bothered you.

Remember the following pattern:

STIMULANT >>>>THOUGHT>>>>>ACTION

Eliminate the any negative stimulant before it triggers thinking which leads to undesirable activity. Stimulant is like a small friction, thought is like a detonator and Action is the actual explosion. Ensure to prevent that friction in the initial stage itself by discouraging its growth in the mind. Use Zero Thinking to remove friction by blowing out that unwanted thoughts.

Happy ZT!

CHAPTER 4

Unwanted Desires: Eliminate Them First!

Many missed opportunities, brooding over past mistakes, nurturing new ambitions based on current trends, numerous unfinished tasks and the list simply goes long for many mid aged people who have been striving hard to make a mark in their career or to put it more precisely the failure to fulfill main ambition.

The major problems lie with the too many desires clouding the mind which gets piled up over the years. There are ambitions right from the days of childhood and even after many years, the desire remains unfulfilled. In these circumstances any amount of self-correction or effort will not be fruitful to get any one ambition fully achieved. More frustrations lead to more complexes in the thought. One loses focus on the actual mission and constantly blames the fate for everything. One of the hallmarks of success which I have dealt with it in another chapter is the need to sacrifice to achieve any one major objective. Imagine you have two desires. The one which is at second priority should be effectively sacrificed in order to achieve quality success in the primary one. This is indeed a tough call. It is like having two strong ambitions like becoming a great sports hero and an entrepreneur. One is involved successfully in the business and at the same time has deep interest in the sports as well. In order to achieve more in any one of them requires sacrificing one for the other. If it is not possible to do it then prepare to lose both or some may justify saying that they have effectively balanced the both. However, in order to achieve high one got to focus all their energy into one. You can never reach the shore by having each leg in the different boats. The trapeze artist lets out the swing before catching the other one. If he doesn't then it is impossible to catch the other swing without letting go the one he is holding. The same applies for any ambition as well. You can either lead moderate content life by having varied interests or sacrifice something BIG to get even BIGGER thing in life. In the principles of Zero Thinking, the complete flushing out all thoughts related to your second most desirable thing in order to focus on the primary objective becomes all important. Even if one desire to learn any new skill, the first question that should be whether this skill will anyway useful in achieving our primary objectives. If the answer is No and one wish to learn the new skill for the sake of interest is just a waste of time and money

One may have heard quite frequently about college drop-outs who pursued entrepreneurship or some who quit plum jobs to write a book. Well, they all have succeeded to a fair level by sacrificing something they were 'comfortable' with. To put it simply one got to move from the zone of comfort to the real battle field. Apply Zero thinking by flushing out the comfort factors and focus on the hardest thing of achieving your goal of through concrete action. Get out of comfort zone. Even applying ZT is also an uncomfortable activity but quite sooner one realizes the real benefits of sticking to the habit of flushing out all unnecessary and non-actionable thoughts in the mind. There are people who having achieved their primary goal and have moved on to pick their second most desirable interest in order to relive the past. This they usually do so by retiring completely from their primary activity. It's a luxury to find time and opportunity to go back to your first love. Many household mothers often say how they sacrificed their hobbies and interests for the sake of the family. Once the kids are grown up and commitments are less, they usually begin new life by rekindling their ambition. Their success is mainly due to their steadfast attention to immediate priorities by eliminating the other desires. They achieve success due to this sacrifice (whether forced or natural) and once having reached certain milestone, they go back to their first love. The better and faster one sacrifices, the more are the choices to lead a complete life.

There are no hard and fast rule for this or a guaranteed outcome but the effort is always worthwhile. So, one should stop whining for having to sacrifice so many good things to get to the bigger goal. Keep flushing out unnecessary thoughts and analysis by using ZT to freshen up your thought process.

Happy ZT!

CHAPTER 5

WIN-WIN Negotiation

It is often understood that in any negotiation, the win-win situation provides better deal. There is no parameter to evaluate what is WIN-WIN deal. In any tough negotiation the situation arises where one group concedes some benefits to the other group. No matter how well a negotiation has taken place, there is always dissatisfaction at least among one group. In a win-lose situation where one wins at the expense of the other, the losing party is never happy with the deal. Many political negotiations always end up with one group going out dissatisfied which leads to major confrontation between them.

In a WIN-WIN process, it is believed that if some give and take policy is adopted then the parties concerned will have long lasting relationship. In corporate jargon it can be referred to as strategic alliance or synergy. We will not delve on the methods of negotiation but would try to understand the concept of Win-win. In order to understand how much is the value of a winning deal, it is essential to keep the emotions under control. First, our side should be clear what we are getting and is it worth in the end. How much we need to offer concessions in order to make the opposite party comfortable? If our side worth is clear to us, then it is better to know the reasons of the opposite party to deal with you for a long time association. Are they looking for any specific advantages at your cost? If so, then what is it and how much will those cost us? In this deal who will benefit the most and if not who will lose the most?

In most such negotiations I always lost on crucial areas only to regret it later and it all happened because of bringing emotions into the discussion. In the excitement of going for the win-win situation I tend to offer 'more' than what I gain in return. I grossly misunderstood the term WINWIN and began to get conscious of other party getting fairer deal. In any negotiation, I now concentrate on my own WIN first and then slowly think of offering as little as possible concessions to my opponent.

So, the Zero Thinking plays crucial role in curtailing emotions during negotiations and look for maximizing benefits for my own interest without having to offend the other party. If I feel I got better of my other partner through my negotiating skills, I go back to offer little more concessions and this is what I refer to as WIN-WIN negotiation. In ZERO THINKING, I go by the philosophy of get exploited to exploit. At the end of the day, you got to negotiate to maximize your benefit first before doling out concessions out of enthusiasm. You can neither afford to get angry nor get too concerned on opposite party's position. Empathy is not required everywhere. I apply zero thinking when I negotiate in order to keep my mind free of uncalled emotions so that I have clarity what I require. This isn't any new concept rather one learns through experience. Again in the end, emotions are part of nature and need not be ignored but to understand and interpret it properly.

Two friends cannot negotiate nor families negotiate, it is usually discussions to agree upon something. Similarly, in any negotiation, the family like discussion has no place. Don't get confused between discussions and negotiation.

Happy ZT!!

CHAPTER 6

How to Stay Motivated to Achieve Goals?

Most ambitious people go through enormous amount of stress in achieving their goals. The loftier the goal the harder it is to achieve it. Interestingly, as said earlier some of the great achievers actually do not have any 'ambitious' goals as such and they accomplish out of sheer passion. It is the love for writing that makes few authors to come out with great works of literature. If one nurtures a goal of writing a bestselling fiction, he or she will likely to struggle quite hard to achieve their goal and in most likely cases may be disappointed. The reason for that is the goal itself clouds their creativity and become conscious of their own quality of work. Instead of worrying about the work making it to best seller list, the emphasis should be in involvement for writing without worrying about the end result.

The Zero thinking helps blank your entire thoughts on GOAL and re-directs your thinking towards the path to achieve your goals. The action, the progress and the effort becomes the priority not the goal. The more one is conscious of achieving something, the harder it becomes to accomplish the same. It is this trap that makes many ambitious people in not getting what they actually dream.

The difficulty in setting goals:

If one is not ambitious it is better. You move in life the way the things unfold for you. No big deal to achieve this or that thing. Keep doing your duty on time or even procrastinate at your convenience as long as your meals are ready when you need it. Better stay that way unless something bothers you. It is foolish to compare and create desires out of impulse. If you are jealous on other's achievements and their lifestyle, it is likely that you are developing a desire in your mind. This kind of desire is not an ambition. It is more of greed than achieving something for purpose. The purpose could be your inner passion or an inspiration from other achievers. You don't need to feel guilty of setting up of goals. All you need is sincere purpose to reach for the goals. The stars may not be in your favour and opportunities keep slipping away from you frequently, this leads to frustration periodically. Invoke ZT to blank all your frustrations, doubts and analyse your failures more accurately to see the real cause behind your setbacks and improve upon them. No achievements can be sweeter than those which comes through real struggle, so a setback is actually a task naturally created to sharpen your skills that empowers one to achieve even bigger things in life. This also does not entitle you to feel happy on the setbacks as it will make one weak and passive. There has to be a bit of anger and frustrations before you overcome them for the next step forward. Never make FAILURE a habit. Strive to beat the failure by accepting it first and then demolishing it to progress.

Be aware of the statistics

Only 1% actually reaches those big goals in any field. So, the reality is to beat 99 people out 100 to reach that position. Imagine, a student attempting to write a tough competitive which is written by a million people, he or she has to compete and beat against an odd 990000 to reach that coveted 1% club of 10000 successful candidates. The next 10000 or other 1% (10001 to 20000) are equally competitive candidates but couldn't perform to that level on that given day. So, the odds are if you want to achieve real success, the goal should be to reach the top 500 or 1000 so as to avoid slipping out of the competition. This formula applies everywhere and the solution is not just only effort, talent, focus but also good doze of luck factor. Not all brilliant scientists achieve Nobel Prize. So do not attach too much importance to the GOAL but focus on constant improvement.

There is no end to the competition in the whole life. One may have missed out on getting admission in Ivy League college, but may go on to achieve better career through sheer talent. It is not the college degree or the money that actually defines the success but how you handle your life's journey throughout. Wealthy and well educated parents may fail in putting their children in better position but ordinary parents may successfully do that with smarter effort. The herd mentality should be discarded. Not all start-ups end up successfully. Some may achieve star status due to right positioning and right timing. Those who fail may fail due to various factors. There are blind curves and blind spots, where some caution is needed. The fact is one cannot even pinpoint a blind spot as well. So, at times it's a game of chance. If one is confident of doing something correctly, then the chances of reaching that goal is much easier. Here, the decision to feel confident should be unbiased. There is no place for the emotion. If your idea or plan is bad, then accept it and discard the action. If nothing is working out well, then change the direction. I love one phrase "If one does same thing again and again yet expect different result is a fool". Either change the goal or change the method of reaching that goal.

Zero thinking as repeatedly said is all about flushing out all thoughts and refresh your thinking by putting oneself in the present environment. Accept the situation and keep moving forward. Stop and take rest if necessary, abandon your goal momentarily and relax for some time. After having found some peace within, slowly plan your next action and reignite your passion. Make sure there is some concrete action without bothering about the outcome and make note of progress. Keep applying ZT as often as you can till you refine your thoughts that helps you stay motivated. Happy ZT!

CHAPTER 7

LAW of Karma

Though an eastern concept, it is now universally acknowledged. However, few people don't believe in such theory. There are people whose only agenda is exploitation. They believe on one life and strive to live it fully. They are least concerned on world's problem. Even if they are told, that they are responsible for the misery in the world, they refuse to accept it. Even if they do wouldn't bother about it. They do not feel guilty nor regret for their actions. According to law of karma no one is spared of consequences of their action. Big dictators have died without pain after killing millions of people. These men put others into unspeakable misery, pain and death. What happened to them after they died? Did they go to hell to suffer an unending punishment or have taken a re-birth to suffer for their deeds? We have no idea nor wish to delve into such thing unnecessarily.

Zero thinking does not permit such complex debates which create an emotional disturbance. There are no easy answers for life's complex problems and if some people claim they have it, then most of them are just lying or faking to know the truth. The only truth to know about Law of Karma is that one has to reap what one has sown. Instead of worrying about the world, it is better to take responsibility on one's duty and abide by the law of the land. Zero thinking does not mean blanking your thoughts on your own action but to be balanced in order to take wise decisions. One is at liberty to use or misuse zero thinking for one's own advantage but there are always consequences. Some are least bothered about consequences and they do what they feel like. Few are scared of consequences and therefore, would avoid doing what is wrong. If fear is the reason, then it is absolute cowardliness. If fear rules your mind, then your emotions are playing a role. Doing right out of fear may be good to the whole society but for self it is not a healthy practice. You don't need to do right just because you fear consequences. Fear is just a key to correct your attitude. It is not essential to be on right or wrong side of the law but how courageous one lives. Doing right thing out of courage is the ultimate conduct. No race, no religion and No nationality are superior over others in any manner. It is our validation to say that one group of people is more successful or civilized than others. Just like in jungle, a tiger cannot be a superior animal over others because of its strength. It is just a part of nature that one animal survives by killing other. The human society is also similar. One group exploits and there are large majority who are exploited. Some humans love the domination and are obsessed on their power to control others. God isn't around to see and judge all these. He has simply created natural laws like a software program that runs on its own. An average human life can be 80 years and it is just fraction of a microsecond in comparison to the age of civilization. The tiniest of fraction of time in the whole creation of the universe that spans a human life proves that we have much longer journey beyond life and death. It is not essential to prove it but very easy to guess that there are journeys beyond one's life considering that we are spending only small quantity of time in a single life with respect to the age of universe. We leave it to the imagination of every human to understand that we have a choice to either make a decent living in this gift of life OR spoil it. The one good thing about this life is those who suffer embrace death with grace for they carry hope of better things beyond the end of their life. The rich, privileged and successful may feel satisfied for the life they lived. No human deserves pain and hardship. It is all one's action, attitude, submission and surrender that counts.

Instead of getting angry over wrongdoers for not getting punished, it is better to be grateful to the powers of nature that one is free from doing anything wrong. Remember, those who get punished instantly for doing something wrong is basically saved by the powerful nature from treading on wrong path.

When a person does all bad things yet thrives and goes on to do more is actually heading towards a trap that he or she has no understanding of what lies ahead. YOU ARE LUCKY TO ESCAPE THAT PATH OF UNCERTAINTY. If you are on right path and then YOU HAVE ABOSLUTELY NOTHING TO WORRY WHATSOEVER.

Now, you blank your thoughts to ZERO and bring your emotions under control. Find out what makes you feel guilty and refrain from all those actions and thoughts that activate guilt feel in one. Not doing a good thing is NOT GUILT but doing wrong is. Life has many challenges and those who prefer to be on the right side of moral conduct often face harder challenges. The life of each individual is designed uniquely. The good people are always more confused of continued struggle and their pain increases when they compare themselves with those who lead happier life. The comparison may be unavoidable but the true fact is what one sees as happier life of the other person may not be entirely correct. There is always some pain behind every smile. The moment one stops comparing and instead be grateful for things around, it is easier to cope with any amount of challenges and hardships. Zero thinking is about clearing one's mind of comparison with others including those who suffer more than you. You don't need to feel guilty for those who suffer more, instead extend whatever help if you can. The Law of Karma prevails everywhere and no one can bypass it.

CHAPTER 8

Sense and Stimulation

One of the deadliest interruptions to progress is unwanted stimulation of the senses. There are many people around the world who have tried and applied every possible tip available to excel in life but for some reason they cannot make it. They keep wondering why they lack the ultimate thing to gain break-through. The lesser known people sometimes make it big much to the surprise and envy of others. Is it all game of chance? Or is there a unique preparation required? Some people have wonderful secrets through which they are able to scale up high in life and they are not aware of. They carry that natural talent or gift which helps them. It is quite normal to envy such people. The list is long. In order to give one simple example there are few persons who do not get angry easily and that gives them an edge. Anger destroys many things. This does not mean angry people do not succeed and they succeed by using anger as tool to achieve perfection. For some sex is another stimulant which gives them the motivation to move forward. However, when you talk of seven deadly sins like Anger, lust, greed, gluttony, envy, pride and sloth all provide moderate positive stimulations to accomplish great things in life. This does not mean one needs to practice all these sins to achieve material comforts. They are major impediments to healthy progress. One cannot be perfect in all. A saint may overcome all the above stimulants and an ordinary human has to struggle to keep everything under check. Zero thinking helps in overcoming the above at right situations and the following methods are easier to apply through little practice.

Anger: If empathy is adopted in every walk of life, the idea of anger automatically subsides. You begin to understand the other man's situation and in most occasions there is a sufficient reason to not get angry. This way one can prevent anger getting clouded in one's thoughts and thereby reducing the efficiency. I love the statement by Dwight Eisenhower who was the supreme commander of the Allied forces in World War 2. He was asked about the conduct of Hitler. His reply was "I do not like to think about a man whom I do not like". He wasn't angry with Hitler as he wanted to achieve the objective of defeating him. His thoughts were clear with the Zero thinking on the subject and he was able to achieve it.

Lust: The lust may not be a common problem, but many potential achievers have this weakness. They cannot free their mind of this deadly stimulant. Those who love it and enjoy it to supreme have no issues about their conduct. Some feel extremely guilty of their weakness and try to overcome through many methods but get trapped often out of temptation. They just can't wriggle out of it. ZT provides a way of help. All one need is little courage to blank the thoughts as often as possible. Any external stimulation that triggers the lust needs only one important STEP, just blank the thoughts immediately. This takes some time to achieve perfection through series of effort. Once achieved it stimulates to feel confident and motivated. However, one single achievement may not be enough; it has to become a habit. Zero thinking is an on-going process to get the perfection in overcoming every obstacle in life. The temptation always provides the fodder and one often succumbs to it. This is why the feel of guilt should be overcome by constant effort to practice Zero thinking. First believe no one is perfect and there is no need to feel guilty as they are part of nature. The idea is to enjoy dodging these stimulations and avoid it to rule your thoughts. There is no such thing as harmless pleasure. Only a healthy thought is harmless. Cultivate healthy thought and continue battle out unhealthy ones through Zero thinking. There is no blacksmith who haven't broken his finger. Similarly, human life is always full of slips and falls. Get up and move on.

Greed: The awareness prevailing in today's time is high. The media constantly throws up success stories one after the other. They keep projecting that the only way to feel success in life is to amass wealth and lead a great life. The trick is that the media is highly dependent on these achievers to patronize their company through advertisements. The success may be genuine but the way it is projected appears that no else has achieved it before. There is no harm in having ambition to achieve one's goals even if it is wealth. The only thing required is to run this rat race not with others but self. Instead of dreaming to be recognized by others for your achievements, you should first recognize your own effort and the outcomes. The desires for excess wealth, bigger car or bigger house are all nothing but temptations of greed. It is the PASSION that should drive you to your goal and has nothing to do in possessions. Zero thinking purges all thoughts on material possessions and re-directs the thought towards the action, improvement in effort, betterment of skill and constant motivation despite setbacks.

Gluttony: Food is a great gift and one can enjoy their meal all the time. Exotic foods and variety makes one feel happy. There are some people who love to say that they live to eat only. In some cultures, the food is very important thing in one's life. They spend about 6 hours a day in preparation, arrangement and eating their meal in a single day. If one has the luxuries enjoy it without guilt. However, eating right thing and in moderation is what gets you a great health. Health is wealth. The best way to avoid gluttony is to share and sacrifice your portion of food with others. Get away from the dining table once you feel half full. Share your favourite food with others and enjoy the portion that you have. Gulp a glass of water before you eat or eat fresh salad before a meal. It is stimulant called hunger the real culprit. Besides hunger, it is the constant thought for cravings that cause the desire to eat. Avoid such cravings by postponing the thought or stimulations in the mind. Do this till you sit for the regular meal.

Envy: This is a common thing prevailing with all humans. Even saints are not spared. It is the most unforgivable among all the other sins. Envy hardly hurts anyone except self. Envy clouds one's thoughts with frustration and hate. It is the foundation of any kind of hatred and prejudice. Envy if uncontrolled can lead to violence and war. Envy triggers anger, greed and pride. Since, it causes other three major sins; therefore, it becomes the most unforgivable among all sins. Zero thinking actually targets one's mind to clear all kinds of envy as it has no tangible value in one's life. Champions don't envy their opponents. They learn from them.

Pride: The human race is highly divided with race, religion, creed, language and geography. The beauty of humans is the ability to create great civilization and survive. Even though there are differences and wars between them, the most regions are peaceful except for few internal disturbances. Pride isn't all that bad except if one believes that he or she is superior to other humans. Every culture, language and region has its own reason to feel proud of their roots. The sanity is in appreciating the beauty of nature's creation. However, in this competitive world it is obvious that everyone wants to feel better than others. The sense of pride is injected in tender age unknowingly by the elders. You got study hard and earn good money is what most youngsters are told. Learn to appreciate others wholeheartedly and this gesture clears all sorts of pride. If you wish to be recognized, then begin to recognize others. Never be conscious of doing good things, always do it with complete detachment of any desires. Doing well for the sake of getting good is nothing but greed. It makes no sense but do it anyway since it will make you better person and soon you will realize the truth behind it.

Someone asked what is the secret of improving memory? Stay away from all the above mentioned behaviours especially anger and ego, this will automatically help you recall many things and help one to do much better in life. I improved my memory a lot by just shedding anger as much as possible.

The ZT is one of the ways to discard the above behaviours. Happy Zero thinking!

CHAPTER 9

Relaxation

In the name of relaxations some have the habit of playing few games often. These extracurricular activities are usually termed as healthy alternative in otherwise busy life with never ending workload. Take for example, any sport that brings exercise to the body and mind are surely very productive form of relaxation. Similarly, any other relaxation like watching movies, surfing internet without any objective, watching interesting videos on social media or even playing online games can be moderately good. In contrast, an ambitious person with clear goals in mind hardly has time for any form of recreation. Now, the question is how much one should devote time for recreational activities and what kind of activities that one must choose in order to unwind completely?

Well, it all depends upon one's interest and hobbies. The thing is to identify any such relaxation activity that not only robs precious time but also disturbs focus. There is an interesting example: A scientist working on a critical project may have problems in focussing if he or she loves any mind games like Chess. There is no proof and one may find it absurd on such theory. However, games like Chess have this issue. The hard-core chess players cannot take up another mental activity with same effectiveness as that of Chess. A Chess players mind is always full of moves and counter moves. Just imagine a scientist develops deep interest in chess and suddenly turns focus on some strategic moves and opening theories of the game. He is most likely will have trouble in focussing on his research projects as the mind will be finding new challenge in the game of chess. Some games like chess becomes more serious one rather than a relaxing sport. In such situations, the relaxation transforms into a serious activity with mind finding new form of challenges thus blurring focus on other mind based activity.

It is therefore essential to discard such sport or games which hampers with mind OR play the game for pure fun rather than taking it too seriously. Some games have the attraction of forming a habit. So, think before joining any recreational club and safeguard one's precious time especially for those who are striving to achieve their goals. This is why meditation is considered to be better form of relaxation followed by brisk walk, jogging and other form of physical exercise. One can find games like Football, Cricket, Badminton and Table tennis a better way to get break than indoor games like Chess. Chess sometimes is dangerously addictive game and can suck one into it. It is more of an egoistic game of showing one's mental superiority. They naturally disturb the pattern of thinking which affects other serious issues involving one's profession. Similarly, online games have this tendency to create a tempting habit of playing again and again thus destroying one's focus on other important activity. Chess is my favourite sport and I love playing it often on internet. This is to clear any kind of prejudice I have for this sport. Since, I play this game at moderate level I understand the implications of losing focus on other important activity. It is therefore, I strongly recommend that be aware of your relaxing methods so that you come back refreshed and energetic. The idea is not to feel happy or excited over a win in a competition but to feel calm and satisfied after a break. If you are member of a badminton club, just go and play to sweat out instead of worrying about your progress in the sport and beating your opponents unless you want to become a regular badminton player with competition in the mind. If you are writing a book or playing a professional sport, you got to be ready to sacrifice one thing to achieve success in the other. So next time, if you are involving yourself in a relaxation mode just relax by blanking your thoughts to Zero thinking. Never be too attached to any activity except your important goals. When you are relaxing make sure your thoughts are clear of unnecessary expectations from your leisure activity. Just enjoy the break and come back into your mission feeling fresh and full of energy to resume your duties. Let there be no residue left in the mind from the activities of break.

The break is meant to clear the mind not to refill with another one. Zero thinking is to purge out any emotions that hampers with thinking in general.

In conclusion, if you want to have an easy going life with some leisure and relaxation, then sacrifice your GOALS for a relaxed life than worrying about an ambition. It is one of the reasons that many are not ambitious and want to lead a simple life. If one is ambitious with big goals in mind, then one should consider relaxation as a kind of re-energising one's activity by keeping it to bare minimum indulgence. In order to transform my business, I briefly left the club where I was having good time playing with my friends. The result was I could scale up and strengthened my business to next level. In order to keep physically fit, I did simple exercises at home rather than wasting my time at fitness centre for hours. The idea is TIME IS PRECIOUS if you are on a serious mission. Use Zero thinking to re-focus on the activity.

Happy Zero Thinking!!

CHAPTER 10

Luck

Few secrets of miracle called LUCK

How many of you have said this often in their lives that "I have no luck"?

Is luck something precious that it finds its way only towards few chosen lucky people all the time?

Can one increase the chances of being lucky next time?

Well, there are no guarantees for any outcome as I said in my previous chapters but the quality of outcome increases with increase in effort and preparation. I love the following phrase:

"Chance favours the prepared mind"

A solid preparation always increases the chances of favourable outcome. Some may call it a luck factor but the sincere efforts behind it are the key. Many wouldn't agree with this as they say the efforts were complete but the results were not good.

Is it essential to rain if the weather is cloudy? Like a passing cloud one should not give too much importance to the outcome and practice accepting the same with humility. However, the effort shouldn't be diluted for the mission unless one wants to abandon it. Now, coming to the factor called luck. How can I be lucky the next time? This luck factor needs to be identified.

Is there a term to describe the opposite of word luck? For example, the opposite of night is day or opposite of cold is hot. What about luck? Is there a word to describe the opposite of LUCK? May be the word jinx comes closer. It is either bad luck, unlucky or ill luck but not a specific term for it. It may be coincidence to not find an exact term to describe the opposite of luck.

So next time if you say "I do not have Luck" it means that the sentence itself carries the word luck. The thing is you are not appreciating the word properly. If you say, it's my bad luck; you are sub consciously using the beautiful word called luck in a negative manner. That is all!

One mantra I urge one to use often is

"I'm lucky and will be luckier"

The other one is to understand the ways to enhance luck in one's life.

Your luck factor increases if you discover and sincerely appreciate the existing luck in your life

It is almost saying that count your blessings.

How many of you have experienced the situation called blessing in disguise? Quite often isn't it? Well that is the luck factor. The lady luck is a Goddess who likes to be adored. One cannot see every adverse situation as a lucky one in disguise. A big loss, tragic circumstance or any major setback may not be a fortune in disguise to appreciate but it does carries deep spiritual experience which has no easy explanation. Only time and patience heals such deep wounds. No one is luckier all the time. This reality must be understood before delving into finding the luck factor in one's life.

It is okay if you are unable to accept the luck factor but do refrain from saying anymore on bad luck situation. You lose an important tournament and many of your admirers may say it is hard luck or better luck next time. In such scenario, one's thought should be that "I am still lucky". If age, opportunity and time are on your side then make best use of it to enhance your chances of success. If not then spread your effort for overall development, never give up on any mission that satisfies your soul.

Another situation where some don't find the right opportunity to work their way to success often blame on the luck factor. It is like saying that I am ready to work hard but lack in motivation. Depression, lack of interest, fatigue, low morale and few similar situations at times robs precious moments to move forward in life. This is often referred to bad luck situation. Here the only solution is to find little happiness and small satisfaction through tiny constructive efforts. Even if this is a problem, then it is slightly serious issue and one needs to seek professional help to overcome such chronic depression. However, it is a common problem and one shouldn't feel alarmed on this unless one continues to ignore the situation. Suspend your ambitious programmes till the time you are ready to resume the same.

Apart from this one need to take proper care of health to increase energy levels besides taking professional help in dealing with situations. There are seven days in a week, believe me that there are at least 3 days available in a week to feel motivated and make sure to grab that situation. Mostly, such livelier mood often tempts one to seek leisure and compromise on precious opportunity. Your leisure should follow your productive efforts not the other way around. Weekend outings are not best option to feel motivated so try and look for various other ways to get energised.

My mantra of success is that, in order to accomplish your most important goal; be ready to sacrifice the next best thing that you are passionate about. This is what known as hyper focus. I remember an old friend of mine who became a famous playwright for movies after sacrificing his lucrative career in the corporate world. Interestingly, he was earning just about same but he was enjoying his job a lot. The decision to leave a plum job was a calculative risk but he was fairly confident that he will manage. He didn't dream of any big things but steadfastly pursued his new career without big expectations. After, some initial struggle and with the help of some known friends in the film industry he managed to position himself firmly. More than luck, he was carefully planning his new career by ensuring he had mentors and guides in his new career.

May the lady luck always cast her smile on your life!

The Zero Thinking is about purging out all bad luck factors from the mind. Avoid comparing yourself with others even on the positive side like I am far better off than many. This is because if you cultivate the habit of comparing one loses the focus on self and thoughts wonder all the time. You are neither in pitiable situation nor better off than others. Your position is just unique. So keep focusing on micro improvements. *Most of the times luck is like a shadow on a cloudy day which follows you invisibly. It is just matter of time before the sun shines.*

Say as often as possible the following words:

"I AM LUCKY AND WILL BE LUCKIER"

CHAPTER 11

Pride & Humility

Feeling proud of anything unique is part of human nature.

Is feeling proud of oneself morally right thing to do?

No! It robs of one's humility and replaces it with some kind of arrogance.

Isn't feeling proud actually triggers performance and leads to more success?

Yes, it does but there is a cost one got to pay at some point of time in life.

How can I avoid feeling proud yet improve my effort and performance to achieve higher success?

One got to keep one's pride to oneself and not brag around telling others even if it quite mild and simple. However, there is something called selling oneself which means one got to express themselves about their progress and achievements in order to get recognition. Well, such compelling situations are fine and welcome but it should be dressed with humility.

How can I talk about my achievements and yet maintain that character of humility?

Try and remember everyone who is responsible for your success beginning from your birth. Express gratitude at every step for whatever you are today. Try and use the following sentence while talking about yourself.

"I think I am luckier to reach this place which I feel I don't deserve"

"The world is full of worthy people and not everyone gets fair chance to achieve"

"When time and tide are on your side every little effort gets rewarded"

"Many people work hard and yet don't see desirable results; I think I am just lucky to be here"

There are many such phrases and sentences to stay calm and composed when all lights are focused on you. Cultivate humility as a habit and let it get ingrained into your character. The highest form of devotion is full of humility and gratitude and nothing else. To think the other human is low in any form kills all the good effort and refrain from seeing other human in any kind of negative manner. When you find others not in compatible with good behavior BE LUCKY THAT YOU ARE NOT HIM OR HER!!! Complete your thought by PRAYING FOR HER OR HIM. Pray for the world and pray for the humanity. The world has no borders and the blood is red for most living beings and the pain too is same for all then why inflict pain on someone when you know it hurts? Change the way you look at the world from NOW ONWARDS!!

As said earlier, it isn't easy to cultivate genuine humility instantly. It takes time to form any good habits. The ZT is to flush out again any such thought of unnecessary pride or self-obsession. The presence of pride isn't again any sin or wrong as it is part of the nature. In fact, it is useful at times to keep going on in life and reach for higher goals. The idea is to not delve too much on such thoughts. Lighten your mind with simple thoughts. Appreciate the situation that makes you feel proud and feel thankful always. Pride will become a tiny dot and eventually disappear.

Happy Zero thinking.

CHAPTER 12

Miracles: A Unique Guide to A Fulfilled Life

The Art of Success is the ability to get out of Comfort Zone. The path to failure is the inability to come out of comfort zone. One act of success and another one of failure will only make you feel more unsuccessful. The failure has no permanent place, it has to be challenged and overcome. At times, life throws challenges in form of temptations, weakened decision making, fatigue and low motivation to pull you back into undesirable comfort zone. One cannot avoid falling down on a slippery surface but the whole idea is to find the determination and re-build motivation to get back to feet. The emotions need to be constantly checked. Every effort need not provide fair results. Desperation will not get anything of value. The idea is to keep moving in right direction with right purpose without attaching emotionally towards outcome. *If the journey is undertaken, then the destination is not far.* If you find difficult to believe in yourself, then BELIEVE IN MIRACLES. Miracles happen every day, every moment and it is indistinguishable. Champions convert victories in most trying situations. Fight to the last point. Winning goals are scored in the last few seconds of the game. Those last moments are crucial. Miracles happen but not frequently and cannot be predicted. Believing only on miracles will not yield results, so try and cultivate faith in self as well and most importantly act on the task. Zero thinking is nothing but to believe that the nature will take care of things. The only thing needed is to be prepared for every eventuality. Human body is a miracle of its own. It has the capacity to heal itself without any aid of medicines. One may notice that the less intelligent and less educated people fare well in life than those who are well educated. The less resourceful rely on nature and most frequently do not bother about challenges that come in their way. Those who graduate from premium institutes usually end up in the golden trap of plum job whereas those from lesser known institutes have to face the rough weather of unemployment or low paying jobs. However, those who face the early challenges usually end up doing better in the later part of their lives. Some even become more successful than their well-educated counter parts. I remember a story during World War 2 when three persons were recruited for various jobs in the Army. Two were school dropouts whereas the third one was an engineer. No wonder, the engineer was promptly recruited as he was expert in overhauling diesel engines. The other two had to wait for few days before being taken up for some menial jobs. Many years later, the two school dropouts were heading various divisions whereas the engineer continued to overhaul the engines. There is no end to miracles and it happens throughout the life.

Zero thinking (ZT) does not ask you to look for the miracle instead it guides you to believe in self and move on with action. The pandemic could have been any more severe and serious but miraculously it nearly disappeared or under effective control. We still wonder how it happened in the first place and how it came under control. Though, effort to control and curb the calamity was fully undertaken by various governments besides the support staff comprising of doctors and nurses whose selfless service being the key, the overall result was miraculously good enough to save the world.

However, miracles are not a dependable allies and so don't waste time expecting it to happen. The effort needs to be one hundred percent to achieve anything. Happy Zero Thinking!

CHAPTER 13

Decisions and the Outcome

There are 4 different categories of decisions:

1. Decision taken equates to desired outcome

2. Decision taken does not equates to desired outcome

3. If 2, then the decision to accept the outcome and move beyond it

4. The decision to not accept the outcome or outright rejection.

Of all the above, the most successful people experience the category 2 & 3 quite commonly which means that not all decisions result in desired outcome. The category 1 represents fulfilled ambition whereas the 2 is just the opposite.

The people who are stubborn usually prefer category 1 and if the decision happens in outcome not desirable then they reject the outcome. This means that there is no room for acceptance of the outcome which is not as per their wish. They are obsessed with category 1 and move to category 4.

Some of the life's biggest blunders happen when a decision maker expects the category 1 situation and if the result is category 2 then he or she refuses to consider category 3 situations. The category 3 is the most powerful based on the LAW OF ACCEPTANCE. Many will not agree with this as it represents compromise on principles. Category 4 is not bad all the time. For example, if you order for vegetarian dish and the waiter says they have only non-vegetarian dishes available, it is obvious that the decision maker will opt for category 4 rather than compromise on the choice. However, the choice of choosing 3 or 4 depends on situation. For example, if one order for coffee and the person in the counter says that they have run out of coffee and instead offers to give fresh fruit juice, the decision maker accepts the juice then the person has used category 3 situations. He or she may even feel that the fresh fruit juice was better choice than coffee since it is a healthier drink. At times, the law of acceptance provides wholesome fulfilment or even more profound positive effect compared to rejection. An ambitious student wants to pursue for competitive exam again after the 1st failed attempt only to find the going difficult whereas another failed student prefers to accept the outcome and pursues his or her education in the college where he or she gets the admission. One sacrifices a year to get what he desires and the other prefers the acceptance of outcome and carries on further. On most occasions, the more satisfied persons usually come from the category 2&3 situations rather than the category 1&4. The sacrifice of a year may give that student an edge in his career since he gets admission in a prestigious institute in comparison to the one who prefers accepting the result as it comes. These are not uncommon. However, as mentioned in the beginning the real success and overall fulfilment happens only to those who give consideration to category 3 rather than 4. The Law of attraction is just an exercise but the ability to move forward comes from law of acceptance only. Success is divided into two types whereby one that of fulfilment and the other that of progress. It is individual's choice whether to enjoy one-night celebrity status or look for long term success. Most of the time, the category 1&4 usually end up frustrated whereas the category 2&3 enjoy more contented life. At times, the biggest successes come to mostly persons who believe in law of acceptance than desperation. There is a difference between working towards goal and working for passion. Athletes and other sports persons usually have to work towards achieving goal like winning medal in Olympics. The real winners are those who forget the goal momentarily and put the passion in their work. The passion to run quicker in a 100-meter dash is better than obsession to win Gold in the Olympics; the latter would follow if everything goes well. The same applies to other areas. Most Nobel laureates wouldn't have dreamt of winning the coveted prize until they got it. The idea is to focus on work not on goal. Apply zero thinking if the goal becomes central part of your thought and blank it to focus on the mission.

Few facts of good decisions:

Ask which is a good and bad decision, like is it beneficial to rise early OR late? The answer is obvious and hence it is quite clear what decision is supposed to be taken. It is up to the individual whether he prefers bad decision to the good one, all for the temptation to be little lazy.

Always weigh between good and the bad. Take the good decision because the bad decision will lead to missed opportunity, loss of reputation, loss of money and so on. At times, the postponement of decision can prove lot beneficial. It depends on situations. I have very inefficient customers whose last minute changes creates problems for me as I hurry up on the project due to time constraint. All my efforts including that of my team goes waste due to change in the specifications. However, some decisions need to be taken fast for better results and efficiency.

Assumption is the mother of all the goof ups. No decision is good which is based on assumption. Many times it can prove costly. It is wise to verify facts before any good decision. Good and accurate decisions based on thorough study of facts is ideal. The carpenter's formula: Measure twice and cut once. I say in today's circumstances, measure four times by engaging another person to do the same. Compare the study and take the decision. A mistake robs precious time, money and most importantly reputation. An efficient outcome with quality weigh more than the time consumed. So, avoid rushing even if the pressure mounts on you as at the end of the day, the real validity will be done on the output of the work. Few may get away with quicker work with moderate results but the one who consistently delivers quality output becomes the Mr. dependable. This however, does not mean that one takes unusually longer time to achieve, the speed also matters at time. IMPROVE QUALITY AND OUTPUT TIME proportionately. I love the Japanese term KAIZEN (continuous improvement).

Keep your thoughts free of unnecessary events or imaginations. Seek expert's opinion especially an experienced one when it comes to critical decisions. Don't leave it to chance or guess work while taking any decision.

CHAPTER 14

24x7 Meditation for 365 Days.

Sounds ridiculous isn't it?

How long should one do meditation?

The answer could be few minutes to an hour OR even more. Some monks, saints and sadhus roaming near Himalayas may be doing it as mentioned above almost throughout the time they breathe. Is it possible? Well, yes!

One should understand the types of meditation. The yogic based meditation with breathing techniques shouldn't be done for longer duration. The meditation which I am talking about is nothing but a complete transformation of self. You begin to accept your complete present status no matter what the situation is. You begin to stop judging others, situations and other stuff that constantly bombards your brain on day to day basis. You numb yourself without losing attention and focus on regular activities.

You begin to view your spouse and your boss in totally different angle. Why spouse and boss comparison?

This is because both of them play very vital role towards your psyche and mood. The 24x7 meditation talks about how you balance your mental position to prevent the following:

They are Anger, Jealousy, Insecurity, Frustration, Fear and Anxiety. These six idiots would ruin anyone's life if left unchecked. There is no need to feel guilty for any of the above situations as it may come uninvited but you got to send them off gracefully. You should neither resist them nor welcome them but redirect them to exit door. This is Zero Thinking. You are neither judging nor analyzing but simply focusing on immediate situation. You should quickly recognize one or more of these idiots at your doorstep before you turn them away.

When you begin to do this regularly and effectively, then you are on 24/7 meditative position. You do not actually need to do any other sophisticated meditation to maintain your inner tranquility. However, an added meditation whereby you silently sit in prayer chanting mantras or even sitting quite will always be helpful. At times life hits a bend and you need some extra care to face the situation. I will never say do not worry. If situation creates worry and fear it has to be ACCEPTED for natural reasons. Shout if you need to or cry if situation demands. These emotional disturbances aren't harmful always but on the contrary shake the person from an unstable position to a stable one. If one maintains unusual calm and tries to overcome through artificial methods by suppressing real feelings, it only creates imbalance which are harmful. I do not recommend to do mediation unless one is completely free of painful and disturbing thoughts.

The one way to flush out such thoughts through ZT is to ask yourself "Will these disturbances in my mind cause any ill health"? The most likely answer is YES. It is therefore, essential to clear your mind by removing those negative stimulations that is constantly hurting you. As they say, that anger is a self-punishment, then why allow it to dominate? The one thing to remember always is that NO ONE CAN GET AWAY hurting another unjustly. Be it physical or mental no one has right to hurt or humiliate or cheat another person. Some may call it law of karma but the fact is EVERY ONE HAS TO PAY FOR THEIR DEEDS. There are stories going around whereby it is told that a small group of people are controlling everything in the world. How far is it true is not the question, but are these people some kind of immortal? As said an average human life span is about 75 years which is just a fraction of time in comparing to the age of earth. One has a choice to do whatever in that 75 years of period. Either one makes a positive impact out of this tiny period of life OR blow-up it all together. Always say that you are lucky that you are not born in a family that thrives in doing things wrong way. It is not important that one pays for his or her deeds but to be satisfied with the beautiful gift of life. One shouldn't waste time in validating who is controlling your life as it is mostly imaginative. The nature is the real master in the end. We are still in the evolution period as life will get better and better with time. It has to be multiple births or some kind of unending journey. Believe to see more beautiful worlds in this big universe. Now, focus back on the mediation. Your thoughts should be in the immediate surroundings and focus on the next course of action. Don't get excited to give lectures to others, keep those excitement and enlightenment to yourself. Just guide others if needed. Now, clear your mind and take a deep breath two or three times. Feel the emptiness of the mind.

Happy Zero thinking!!!

CHAPTER 15

Keep Fit

Are you jobless and having free time? Is this bothering you and you are running around in search of work? Do you resent doing household chores in this spare time and make you feel restless? Is the routine work make you feel demotivated due to lack of job? This is natural. When something very big bothers you like not having a job, the resultant stress make one feel disinterested in doing anything be it creative or routine important tasks.

Actually spare time is luxury. How many of you would agree that the during the pandemic, the spare time was effectively put to good use?

A busy person has more time than the lazy one. This is quite true, when a person is busy doing some work he or she usually tries to do many other odd jobs as well. A lazy person stretches a work in hand so much that he assumes he is busy and has no time. In fact, he is lazy basically and inefficient as well. A busy person is more organized and every completed tasks motivate him or her to do another one.

What can be done effectively during free time?

First assess how free you are. Do you have that spare time in the morning or in any other part of the day? Accordingly plan your free time for some useful tasks. Learn new skills that will come handy especially in fixing things at home. Today, many DIY videos are available to learn. Make the best use of free time to STAY FIT. Physical exercise is the best form of improving self. Nothing can beat a good physical exercise. It is not simple stretching or bending at your convenience but actually feeling the mild pain while performing any physical exercise. No gain without pain as they say. One should find sufficiently tired after a good exercise. Know your body well. Do not attempt to match your physical fitness programs with others. Discover your strength and limitations before attempting to do any hard exercise. Start slowly with warm up walk and gradually increase your time.

Practice the art of taking GOOD DECISIONS (as mentioned in Chapter 13). Ask every time which is the good decision. Is it good to get up early? If you feel yes, then DO IT. Which is good? Is it going for daily exercise OR just simply sitting idle? Take that Good decision as often as possible. Always weigh, what is good or bad and once known, then take that decision. Don't bother about any bad decisions that one would have taken instead assess why you took that decision. Learn through experience and ensure not to repeat it again. At times, bad decisions lead to better results and vice versa. However, that can never be a benchmark. It is the prepared decision and planned effort that leads to desired results. Practice the art of improving 1% every day in any chosen areas.

Happy ZERO Thinking!!